# Finding a Job and Paying Taxes

Other titles in the *Money and Finance Guide*
series include:

Building a Budget and Savings Plan
College and Career Planning
Managing Credit and Debt
The Value of Stocks, Bonds, and Investments

*Money and Finance Guide*

# Finding a Job and Paying Taxes

Carla Mooney

ReferencePoint Press

San Diego, CA

LIBRARY OF CONGRESS CATALOGING-IN-PUBLICATION DATA

Names: Mooney, Carla, 1970- author.
Title: Finding a job and paying taxes / by Carla Mooney.
Description: San Diego, CA : ReferencePoint Press, Inc., 2021. | Series:
  Money and finance guide | Includes bibliographical references and index.
Identifiers: LCCN 2020034072 (print) | LCCN 2020034073 (ebook) | ISBN
  9781678200541 (library binding) | ISBN 9781678200558 (ebook)
Subjects: LCSH: Teenagers--Employment--United States--Juvenile literature.
  | Job hunting--United States--Juvenile literature. | Wages--United
  States--Juvenile literature. | Income tax--United States--Juvenile
  literature. | Vocational guidance--United States--Juvenile literature.
Classification: LCC HD6273 .M66 2021  (print) | LCC HD6273  (ebook) | DDC
  650.140835/0973--dc23
LC record available at https://lccn.loc.gov/2020034072
LC ebook record available at https://lccn.loc.gov/2020034073

# Contents

# Valuable Experience

When he turned sixteen years old, Jaden Deal started a job at a local restaurant near Des Moines, Iowa. At first, Deal worked in an entry-level position as a host and bussed tables. Now he works fifteen to twenty hours a week as a server at the restaurant while also attending high school. Deal enjoys earning a paycheck and helping out at home with expenses. "The pay is good, and the tips are even better," he says. "I'm able to come [home] after work and help my dad to pay bills or buy groceries. It's just the two of us living together, so anything extra I can help provide makes all the difference."[1]

Deal's part-time job also gives him valuable experience and skills that will help him succeed in college and beyond. Before he started working, Deal did not find it easy to talk to people he did not know well. Now his work experience has made him much more comfortable dealing with new people. "I feel like I've developed 'people skills' from working in the restaurant industry," he says. "I can make small talk a lot more easily and I've learned more about my community by talking with the people I'm serving."[2] Deal plans to continue working as a server after he graduates from high school and while he attends college.

Like Deal, millions of teens across the United States work in a variety of jobs. According the Bureau of Labor Statistics, 21.2 million sixteen- to twenty-four-year-olds were employed as of July 2019. These teens and young adults are employed in roles from waiters and cashiers to child care workers and lawn care specialists. Some teens even operate their own businesses.

> "I feel like I've developed 'people skills' from working in the restaurant industry. I can make small talk a lot more easily and I've learned more about my community by talking with the people I'm serving."[2]
>
> —Jaden Dean, a teen working as a server

## Benefits of a Teen Job

Beyond a steady paycheck, teens who work gain valuable experience and life skills that will benefit them for years to come. Working a job can help teens learn money management skills as

*Working a part-time job not only provides a steady paycheck but also teaches many life skills.*

well as basic work skills such as creating a résumé, interviewing, and working with different personality types. They can learn about different industries and career fields that might help them decide what jobs and education to pursue in the future. On the job, they also develop self-confidence and a sense of responsibility.

According to Jeffrey Selingo, a professor at Arizona State University, there is no substitute for the experience gained from working a part-time job, even if the job is not in the career field that a teen might ultimately pursue. Part-time jobs teach teens the skills they will need to be successful in the future, such as communication, teamwork, responsibility, and more. "It's where they learn the importance of showing up on time, keeping to a schedule, completing a list of tasks, and being accountable to a manager who might give them their first dose of negative feedback so they finally realize they're not as great as their teachers, parents, and college acceptance letters have led them to believe,"[3] Selingo says. With a little research and preparation, teens who want to work can land a job, start earning a paycheck, and gain valuable experience for their future.

# Chapter One

# Types of Jobs: Where to Start

Across the United States millions of teens are going to work. Some work part-time jobs throughout the year, while others work full-time summer jobs. They work in industries ranging from retail to lawn care. Some even work for themselves.

Teens work for a variety of reasons. Some work to gain experience in a certain field. Others work to earn money that they can use to contribute to family expenses. Some teens spend their paychecks to buy clothes or go out with friends, while others save their earnings for a bigger purchase like a car or vacation. Kyra Kelly, a fifteen-year-old living in the San Francisco Bay Area, decided to get a summer job so she could save money to buy a car. To find a business that was hiring, she checked the websites of local stores that she visited regularly. "I found that an ice cream place was hiring, and I went to their website and signed up,"[4] says Kelly. After the store manager met her for an interview, Kelly landed the job.

## Evaluate Strengths and Interests

Before you start looking for a job, it is a good idea to think about what type of job you want to do. Even for teens, there are a variety of job options. Finding a position that matches your strengths and interests can make it more likely you will perform well and enjoy the hours spent at work.

As you start a job search, consider your interests. Do you love animals? If so, a job at a pet store, at a veterinarian's office, or as a dog walker or pet sitter might be a good fit. Teens who prefer working with kids might look into job opportunities at local camps and day cares or start a babysitting service. Teens who are interested in sports might enjoy working at a sports retail store or as a referee in youth leagues. Teens who are fascinated by fashion can often find jobs in a variety of clothing retail stores. Budding chefs may want to find a job in a restaurant, while future journalists or authors may enjoy working in a local bookstore or library.

It's also a good idea for job-hunting teens to take an honest look at their strengths and weaknesses. Are you introverted or extroverted? Do you like to focus on one project at a time, or can you multitask with ease? Do you get along well with

## Employee vs. Self-Employed

Many teens work as employees of a business. Employees generally have a predictable work schedule and a defined pay rate. If they work a certain number of hours each week, some employees are eligible for benefits such as health insurance, paid vacation time, and other perks. Employees are paid by the company for which they work. The company withholds certain taxes—federal and state income tax, social security tax, and Medicare tax—from an employee's paycheck. The employer pays these taxes to the appropriate government agency.

Some teens choose to be their own boss. They start their own business or work as a freelancer for customers. Unlike employees, self-employed workers often have a more unpredictable schedule. They find their own customers and projects and work as required. They bill customers typically by the hour or by the project. When customers pay them, self-employed workers are responsible for paying their own taxes to the federal, state, and local governments.

young children, or are you more easily able to communicate with adults? Knowing these personal traits can help you determine what type of job will be a good fit for you. "If the job involves speaking skills and [you aren't] comfortable with that kind of interaction, the job may not work out in the end,"[5] says Nadia Conyers, a workforce development specialist with Arlington County, Virginia.

For example, teens who are introverted may not feel comfortable working in a customer-facing role such as a cashier, server, or retail sales associate. Instead, they may be better suited for a job in which they have less contact with customers. Teens who enjoy talking to strangers and are good at multitasking may do well as a server, because they will constantly interact with new people and juggle multiple orders at a time. "Investing the time upfront to self-evaluate allows you to be more targeted, and therefore more efficient, when networking and applying for jobs because you know what you want and what you have to offer," says career management coach Kathleen Brady. "The hardest part is getting started," she adds. "People get stuck when they aren't clear what they are passionate about or what their values are. So start by examining something tangible and measurable . . . your skills and abilities."[6]

> "Investing the time upfront to self-evaluate allows you to be more targeted, and therefore more efficient, when networking and applying for jobs because you know what you want and what you have to offer."[6]
>
> —Kathleen Brady, a career management coach

## Working Outside

Teens who enjoy the outdoors might look for a job that allows them to spend long hours outside. Some teens find jobs mowing lawns, gardening, mulching, and performing other lawn care projects. They might work for an established lawn care company or start their own lawn care business and build a list of clients from neighbors who need help with their lawns. Looking to the future,

Summer jobs are a great way to earn an extra income and create new networking opportunities.

working in lawn care is great experience for someone interested in a career in landscape design.

Fifteen-year-old Caleb Tippetts from Burton, Idaho, has been working mowing lawns since he was eleven. After getting his start mowing his family's lawn, Tippetts liked it so much he decided to turn it into a business. "I've always liked being outside working. It just kind of came to me (to mow lawns). It was really fun," he says. "I just love being out there and doing stuff rather than sitting inside doing nothing. It's really fun to be outside and to be in nature." Currently, Tippetts mows lawns for eight customers. "I'm hoping for more. I want to get around 20,"[7] he says.

Some teens work outdoors at a golf course. They fill roles in the day-to-day operations at the course. They greet guests, clean carts and other equipment, and perform maintenance on carts and the course. Golf caddies carry bags for golfers and assist them as they play the course.

Teens who enjoy the outdoors and are accomplished swimmers can get a job as a lifeguard. Many pools need lifeguards during the summer months and hire local teens. To get a job as a lifeguard, people often need training in first aid and cardiopulmonary resuscitation (CPR). They must also have earned a lifeguard certification, which ensures they are properly trained in case of a water emergency. Other jobs that entail spending many hours outside include working for a local park or nature reserve, washing cars, and painting houses.

## Working with Children

For some teens, channeling their inner child and working with kids can be a great job. Teens who interact well with children can pursue a variety of jobs that allow them to spend most of their time with little ones. For example, many summer camps hire teens as counselors. These camps can be day camps or overnight camps. Often, they cater to specific interests, such as a camp focused on outdoor adventure or computer coding. Emma Steinert is a counselor at Circus Smirkus Camp in Greensboro, Vermont. "After being a camper for six years, I knew that the summer I was old enough to work, I wanted to apply," she says. "Working now as a counselor is my way of giving back after so many years of receiving the 'magic' that camp offers and doing my best to create my own magic for kids. Working alongside some of my best friends that I grew up with at camp makes it all the more meaningful."[8]

"Working now as a counselor is my way of giving back after so many years of receiving the 'magic' that camp offers and doing my best to create my own magic for kids."[8]

—Emma Steinert, a counselor at Circus Smirkus Camp in Greensboro, Vermont

Many teens who work well with kids take jobs as babysitters. Some prepare for babysitting by taking a class through the Red

Cross or local YMCA to learn the essentials of caring for children and of basic first aid. Babysitters can work regular hours for a single family or have a collection of families for whom they work. "Because children are so open and have fewer barriers and morals and preconceptions about the world, they love so easily and purely. You can listen to their story for two minutes and you become their favorite person in the universe. I love this job because I love listening. Kids are often in need of someone who cares enough to listen,"[9] says Ari, a seventeen-year-old babysitter.

If you are strong in a particular subject in school, you may find a job as a tutor for children. Tutors meet with their clients on a regular basis to go over assignments, answer questions, and provide enrichment activities in subjects from math and reading to biology and Spanish. A school guidance counselor or teacher can connect teens with younger students who need help. Teens may also work at a tutoring center that offers a variety of help for many students.

## Working with Animals

Have you been taking care of family pets for as long as you can remember? If so, a job with animals and pets may be ideal. Some teens work as pet sitters and take care of animals when clients go out of town for work or vacation. They may take care of the pet in their own home or in their customer's home. Some teens work as dog walkers. They take the dogs out for regular walks and playtime when the owners are at work or away from home for several hours. Teens often start out as pet sitters or dog walkers by taking jobs from people they know. They can advertise their services to neighbors, family, and friends and build a list of clients.

Local farms or ranches may also employ teens. When Andrew Corrigal of Abbotsford, British Columbia, Canada, was thirteen years old, he rode his bike after school to a local farm to help out with a few chores. Soon after, he landed a summer job baling hay

Many teens find working with animals to be rewarding and fun.

and cleaning barns. Corrigal's work on the farm sparked his love of agriculture. He is currently in college pursuing a degree in agricultural technology. "If it hadn't been for that first job, I wouldn't have discovered I love working around animals," he says. "My dream is to become a rancher."[10]

## Working with People

Customer service jobs offer teens who are outgoing and enjoy interacting with a variety of people a good fit. Teens may choose to work as a server or host in a full-service or fast-food restaurant, where they can gain experience working with the public.

Servers are the main contact between the customer and the restaurant's kitchen. They take orders, deliver food and drinks, and make sure that each customer's needs are met. Some restaurants are fast paced and move customers in and out quickly. Others are slower-paced and more formal.

Because servers constantly interact with customers, they should have strong people skills. They should be friendly, helpful, and able to engage in small talk. They are also good listeners and able to take customer orders and correctly send them to the restaurant's kitchen. For teens who are a little shy but still enjoy the restaurant atmosphere, a behind-the-scenes job as a dishwasher may be a good fit.

Retail stores also offer jobs for teens who enjoy interacting with customers. "The best sales people are those who can relate to others, show genuine interest in others, and can share their real voice when they speak,"[11] says Christina Markadakis, a sales talent recruiter at the career website the Muse. Teens can look for jobs in stores that match their interests, such as fashion, sporting goods, computers and technology, or books. Some find jobs in big retailers that sell multiple types of products or at grocery stores. In a retail job, teens stock shelves and arrange store displays, work as cashiers, clean public areas, and help customers find the products they need.

Other customer service jobs include movie theater attendant, recreation center or amusement park attendant, office receptionist or administrative assistant, and barista in a coffeehouse. Hunter McVae, a high school student in New York State,

## Blogging on *Teens Got Cents*

When Eva Baker was sixteen years old, she started a blog, *Teens Got Cents*, that focused on teaching teens to be smart about how they use money. As a homeschool student, Eva started the blog as an assignment given to her by her teacher and mother, Charlotte. Eva's mother wanted her daughter to work on a senior project that involved real-world communications. Eva decided to focus her blog on personal finance for teens after realizing there were few similar resources available for young people. Although she worked hard on the assignment, she first thought of the blog as simply that, a school assignment. However, the blog quickly became popular, and Eva found herself receiving paid offers to teach personal finance classes and become a brand ambassador for a local credit union. Within two years of the blog's launch, it had become Eva's full-time business. The blog has enabled her to network within the personal finance community and book paying jobs as a brand ambassador, speaker, and educator. She's also started adding traditional blogging revenue streams like affiliate marketing to her site. Today, Eva earns more than $5,000 per month from her freelance business.

works as a recreation attendant at a local pool. "My favorite thing about having a job is meeting new people and making friends, along with being occupied with work,"[12] he says.

## Working Online

With a computer and internet connection, some tech-savvy teens find a job working online. For those who are skilled at designing and building websites, they can use those skills to help others. To get started, you may want to design and build some websites for a local charity or family member. You can use these online examples to show off your skills to potential clients.

Similarly, some teens earn money working as online freelance graphic designers. They use their art and computer skills to design logos and create custom graphics for customers. They might create business cards, design T-shirt graphics, or design logos for local youth sports teams. Some talented teens sell their work through online websites like Fiverr or Upwork. Other creative teens make and sell items online like jewelry, pottery, paintings, clothing, T-shirts, wooden toys, and more. They can also sell objects they have made through sites like Etsy.

For teens who are not as craft-oriented, online blogging is another way to earn some extra money. Teens can create a niche blog on a topic that interests them and others. As they get more followers, they can earn money from affiliate links.

In a similar way, online influencers who have a lot of social media followers get paid by companies to promote their products online. Kim, a thirteen-year-old from New York City, charges brands twenty dollars for a permanent post in her Instagram feed

*Tech-savvy teens are finding jobs working online; from social media to graphic design, online experience can create limitless opportunities for the future.*

and ten dollars for a post that she deletes after twenty-four hours. "I thought this might be a good way for me to make money over the summer," she says. "Usually all I do over the summer is sit at home. It's hard to find jobs that take kids at my age, so this is the best option for me."[13] Deanna, a sixteen-year-old from California, says that partnering with brands on her Instagram account allowed her to make some extra money while she worked on college applications over the summer. She plans to use the money she's earned online to buy her college textbooks. "I know a lot of people think that social media is a cop-out, but I think it's a totally valid way to make extra money on what's trending right now," Deanna says. "Trends come and go. There's honestly no reason why we can't monetize what's popular and what people are interested in."[14]

## Building Valuable Skills

As a working teen you can learn valuable skills that will serve you well in the future. Working helps you build your confidence, self-esteem, and independence. You learn how to manage your time, work with others, and communicate with a variety of people. You can also gain experience in areas that may become a future career. Whether you are looking for a part-time or summer job, there are many job options. By doing a self-assessment of your strengths and interests, you can give yourself the best chance to find a job that will be a great fit.

# Chapter Two

# The Job Hunt

For many teens, the idea of looking for a job is daunting. How do you know who is hiring? What makes a good employee? How should you approach potential employers? What should you say to convince them that you are the right person for the job? Looking for your first part-time job may seem overwhelming. You've never worked in a real job before and don't know where to start. Although it can be a challenge, with a little preparation, finding a job can be done.

## Informational Interviews

If you've already done a self-assessment, you've got a pretty good idea of your strengths and weaknesses, as well as your interests. Now you can take that information and see how it matches real-life jobs and companies. You might think you'd be a great dog walker, but have you talked to someone who knows firsthand what the job entails?

Informational interviews can help. Chatting with someone who works in a job or for a company that you are interested in can help you get a better understanding of the work. While you may feel a bit awkward asking complete strangers about their work, they will usually be glad to help. Most people enjoy talking about their job and passing along advice to teens exploring different jobs. "People want to be helpful," says Phil Blair, who is an executive officer of Manpower, a nationwide staffing company. "You might ask to call them later to make an appointment to come by their office, or to meet them at the soccer field early next week, or after work one day next week."[15] Wendy Marcinkus Murphy, an associate professor of management at Babson College, agrees. "When you're a student you have permission to ask questions," she says. "People are happy to help students, particularly when they see a genuine curiosity. The rejection rate is very low. Most adults love to talk about themselves. It's usually easy to get someone talking if you're prepared with good questions."[16]

To get started, do some preliminary research in the library or online about potential job areas and employers that you want to learn about. Then you can start identifying people to interview. You might have a family member or friend who works in the job. Or you may know someone who has a contact that can help you find a person to interview. Before you contact the person, take some time to plan out the questions you want to ask. When you reach out by email or phone, introduce yourself and mention how you got the person's name. Explain that you are not looking for a job but want to learn more about his or her position. You can ask whether the person has time to talk now or would rather schedule a time later to speak with you. Take notes during your conversation so you remember the important details. Afterward, send a note or email to thank the person for his or her advice and time.

> "When you're a student you have permission to ask questions. People are happy to help students, particularly when they see a genuine curiosity."[16]
>
> —Wendy Marcinkus Murphy, an associate professor of management at Babson College

These types of interviews allow you to get firsthand information about what it's really like to work in a job, industry, or company. You'll hear about the positives of a job and also what's not so great about it. This kind of information is valuable and not always easily available online. You might even find out about related jobs

*Going to an informational interview gives a clear and realistic view of what the job entails.*

that you had never considered. Informational interviews can also help you gather insider tips and knowledge about how to prepare for and land your first job. You'll learn what it is like to work for a specific company, and you might meet someone who can be a contact that leads you to a job in the future.

## Labor Laws

Across the country, state and federal laws set rules for teen workers. Before you look for a job, you need to understand the laws for your state and how they apply to you. Under federal law, fourteen is the minimum age for employment. In addition, teens under age sixteen are limited in the number of hours they can work and what jobs they can do. Fourteen- and fifteen-year-olds can work no more than three hours on a school day and no more than eighteen hours per week when school is in session. When school is not in session, fourteen- and fifteen-year-old workers can work no more than eight hours per day and no more than forty hours per week. In addition, they may not work before 7:00 a.m. or after 7:00 p.m. on any day, except during the summer when they can work as late as 9:00 p.m. There are a few exceptions to age-based work restrictions when minors are working for their parents or guardians. For teens under age eighteen, federal law also prohibits minors from working in jobs declared hazardous, such as operating many types of power-driven equipment, mining, excavation, and the manufacturing of explosives.

## Networking

It's never too early to learn the skill of networking. Networking occurs when you interact with others to exchange information and develop social or professional contacts. It can help you make connections that will help you as you look for a job, apply to college, or start a business. Don't worry if this prospect makes you nervous—almost everyone feels anxious about talking to new people. For many people, the scariest part of networking is starting the conversation. To overcome this, you can start by offering a simple handshake and introducing yourself. Often, that's all you need to get a conversation started. Bringing a friend along who is interested in the same career field can also help calm networking nerves and boost your confidence. You and your friend can take turns in a conversation, which reduces the burden on both of you. Networking and developing connections take time. Not every networking opportunity will be a success, but you shouldn't let that stop you from approaching the next opportunity. You never know when you will meet a person who will become a valuable contact for the future. Just like anything that you have done in your life, the first time you did it you were nervous. Practice and repetition are the key to getting over the anxiety you may feel over doing something new.

Each state also has its own laws regarding the employment of teens under age eighteen. If state law and federal law conflict, the law that is more protective of the minor applies. In addition, many states require teens under age sixteen to provide an employment certificate or a work permit. You should make sure you know which, if any, your state requires.

## Who's Hiring?

Once you have a better idea of the type of job you want and the labor laws that apply, you are ready to find out whose hiring and what type of workers they want. There are many avenues that teens and adults use to discover open jobs. One of the best ways is to lean on a network of people you know. Do any of your friends have jobs? Talk to them and see whether their employers are hiring. What type of workers are their employers looking to hire? Does your friend like his or her job? If so, your friend might be willing to introduce you to his or her supervisor.

### Make a Backup Plan

If you have tried a number of things and still didn't land that summer job, don't give up! Instead of sitting home and sulking, make sure you have a backup plan. If you don't find the job you want, make one for yourself. You can become an entrepreneur and gain valuable work and business experience. Many young entrepreneurs get their start providing services for others, such as lawn mowing, dog walking, pet sitting, babysitting, tutoring, computer help, or sports training. You can advertise your services through flyers, social media, and word of mouth.

Other teens decide to volunteer and earn community service hours. There are a variety of opportunities for teens with different community organizations, hospitals, government agencies, and local charities. As a volunteer, you can gain experience and connections that may lead to a paying job in the future.

Your parents might also know local businesses that are hiring. Reach out to your neighbors, teachers, counselors, coaches, youth ministers, and family members to tell them about your interest in finding a job. They might have suggestions for employers or people to approach. As a bonus, potential employers might be more willing to hire a teen who comes recommended by a trusted adult. When teenager Jonny volunteered at a local animal shelter, he impressed the adult volunteers so much that they offered him a paying job at a local Italian ice franchise they owned. "You never know who people know,"[17] says Lisa Kennely, Jonny's mother.

What if you don't have a lot of people to ask for advice? Networking experts recommend getting involved in school and community activities. You can play sports, join the drama club, or volunteer for a local charity. All of these activities will expand your circle of people who may be able to help in a future job search. "Join the debate team, play sports—I don't care what the sport, it can be bowling, it can be anything as long as you're involved in teamwork," Blair says. "It can be your church. It can be the YMCA. It can be the Boys and Girls Club. It doesn't have to be school."[18]

> "I knew I wanted to work in the food service industry, but I didn't really want to work in a sit-down restaurant."[19]
>
> —Seventeen-year-old Ben Hosansky, who found a summer job at Chipotle Mexican Grill in Louisville, Colorado.

Many teens learn about open jobs by visiting potential employers. You might visit your favorite restaurant or clothing store and see a help-wanted sign in the window. Teens can also search for open positions online. Many businesses post open jobs on their websites. Specialized job search websites like Indeed allow users to search and filter results based on certain criteria. "I knew I wanted to work in the food service industry, but I didn't really want to work in a sit-down restaurant," says seventeen-year-old Ben Hosansky, who found a summer job at Chipotle Mexican Grill in Louisville, Colorado. "I applied to a number of fast casual places, including Chipotle, and they were the first to set up an interview."[19]

## Job Fairs

Many communities organize job fairs specifically aimed at teens and young adults. Often held in March and April, these events bring together hiring employers and job-seeking teens. Teens can talk to a variety of potential employers to learn about their businesses and open positions and fill out job applications on-site. Some job fairs are in person, while others are online.

In Pueblo, Colorado, the Pueblo Workforce Center hosts the annual Youth Employment Expo each spring. Open to teens and young adults ages fourteen to twenty-four, the event is free for job seekers. At the job fair, more than forty-five local employers participate. Teens can apply for jobs, meet with employers, and enroll in the Governor's Summer Job Hunt program, which is a state-wide effort to match young workers with hiring employers. Hiring employers include manufacturers, warehouses, retail stores, restau-

*Job fairs allow you to learn about available opportunities that match your interests.*

rants, and the city and county parks and recreation departments. "That's what is nice. Ideally, they just want to get plugged into the workforce center. We do all of the looking for them and we have a variety of jobs,"[20] says Rob Martinez, the Pueblo area coordinator of the Governor's Summer Job Hunt program.

"You generally don't just walk in and get hired. In this generation of immediate gratification, expectations can be unrealistic."[21]

—Nadia Conyers, a workforce development specialist with Arlington County, Virginia

## No Instant Gratification

Finding a job is not always quick and easy. You'll need to take the time to investigate potential jobs and employers and search for open positions. Finding a job and getting hired won't happen overnight. Instead, finding a part-time or summer job is a process. "You generally don't just walk in and get hired," says Nadia Conyers, a workforce development specialist with Arlington County, Virginia. "In this generation of immediate gratification, expectations can be unrealistic,"[21] she notes. By being organized and prepared, you'll have the best chance to find the job you want.

# Chapter Three

# Job Application and Interview

When you have done your homework to research jobs, understand labor laws, and find hiring employers, you are ready for the next steps in the job hunting process—applying for a job and interviewing with potential employers.

## Preparing a Résumé

Some employers require job applicants to send in a résumé when they apply for a job. A résumé is a one- to two-page document that lists a job seeker's qualifications. It highlights any previous work experience the person has, as well as the person's educational background, skills, and accomplishments.

There are several pieces of important information a résumé should include. At a minimum, your résumé should include your contact information, such as cell phone and email address. You'll also want to list any work experience that you already have, including the company where you worked, your position, and what your responsibilities were. A résumé should also include your educational background, such as where you go to school and whether you have graduated from high school or college.

If you have no work experience yet, you can still write a résumé that will let your future employer know who you are. In the education section, highlight any academic accomplishments. Achievements such as a high grade point average or academic awards show that you are successful in the classroom. Employers know that success in school often translates into success at work. If any of your school classes relate to the job you are applying for, you should list them on your résumé. For example, taking a child development class is a good experience to note on a résumé if you plan to apply for a job at a day care, summer camp, or other child-related position.

A résumé is a valuable tool for presenting your skills and accomplishments to potential employers.

List any musical instruments you play, hobbies, and other evidence that you have taken on extracurricular activities that require time and effort. Other activities include sports, clubs, babysitting, and volunteer work. Maybe you play on the school field hockey team or are an active member of the school orchestra or band. These activities are another way to show potential employers your skills, abilities, and dedication. Bruno Delfante, manager at the Small Business Development Corporation in Western Australia, looks for these traits when hiring teen employees. "When recruiting teenagers, good traits to look for include being captain or member of a sporting team, head girl or boy at school, coaching younger children, or being involved in volunteer work. These roles indicate leadership, punctuality, dedication, confidence, and strong interpersonal skills,"[22] he says.

You can also highlight any special skills you have on your résumé. Do you know how to build a website or manage social media accounts? If so, make sure to show that on your résumé. Do you speak another language, have CPR certification, or know computer programming languages? Make sure to list these skills on your résumé.

When you prepare your résumé, online templates can guide you on a simple, standard format that will make it look professional. When you've finished writing your résumé, proofread it carefully to make sure there are no mistakes. Have a friend or family member read it to make sure it is error-free before you send it out to hiring managers.

## Filling Out a Job Application

Some businesses ask potential employees to fill out a job application. Many job applications are online, but some can be paper applications. Regardless of the type of application, you need to make sure you fill it out completely, accurately, and legibly. If information is missing or a hiring manager cannot easily read it, your application may get quickly passed over for another applicant's.

## Typical Interview Questions

While every job is different, many interviewers ask similar questions. They often ask open-ended questions about you to help them learn about your personality and determine whether you are a good fit for the job. If you had a job before, expect questions about it and why you left. You may also be asked questions about why you want the job and why you think you'd be a good fit for the business. Common interview questions and requests include:

- Tell me about yourself.
- What is your greatest strength?
- What is your greatest weakness?
- What makes you unique?
- Tell me something about yourself that is not on your résumé.
- Why should we hire you?
- Why do you want to leave (or why have you left) your current job?
- Why do you want this job?
- How do you handle pressure?
- Describe a difficult work situation and how you handled it.

Leaving off important information can also get your application turned down quickly.

If possible, see if you can pick up the application and take it home to complete it. That way, you'll be able to take your time filling it out completely and correctly. Before you start filling it out, make a list of all of the information you will need to include. Most job applications ask for personal information such as your name, address, phone number, email address, and a work permit if required by your state. The application will also typically ask for your educational history, such as what schools or training programs you have attended; the diplomas, degrees, or certificates you have earned; and graduation dates. You will also need to provide information about any past jobs you have held, including the names, addresses, and phone numbers of previous employers; dates of employment; reason for leaving; and contact information for your previous supervisor. Some applications will ask you when you are available to start working and what days and hours you are available to work.

If you have a résumé, you can use it to help you fill out the information requested in the application. Another option is to look up a standard job application online, fill it out, and use it as a guide to help you fill out a potential employer's on-site application.

Many job applications ask applicants to list their prior work experience. If this is your first job, you can list other types of work that you have done, such as babysitting, yard work, volunteer work, or work with school or community clubs. Make sure to showcase the responsibilities you had in these prior jobs and experiences that would be valuable in the job you are applying for. For example, if you are applying for a job working at a retail store, you can highlight responsibilities that show you have good communication skills, work well with a team, and are organized.

## References

Many employers will ask you to give them the name and contact information for a few references. A reference is a person who will verify that you are a responsible person and good worker. If you have a previous job, you can use a former supervisor as a reference. This person will be able to talk directly about how you performed at work, got along with other employees, and more.

If you've never had a formal job, you can ask people for whom you babysit, dog walk, or mow lawns to be a reference. Other people you can ask include teachers, coaches, clergy members, and other adults who are not related to you and know you well. It is a good idea to ask people to be a reference first before you give their name to a potential employer so they will be prepared to give you a positive recommendation if the hiring manager calls them.

In addition to asking for references, some hiring managers will check potential employees on social media. Sue Bell, who co-owns Melissa and Sue Camps, has interviewed many teenagers for jobs as camp counselors and checks out potential employees on social media. "I will say, and this is a very interesting thing that's only been in the last 10 years of my job, is that I can check these kids up on social media, and I do. And I've not asked for an interview and I've not hired someone because of what I saw on social media," she says. Sometimes, pictures of teens partying or making out will disqualify them for the job. "One in particular, she was writing about how much she hated her job,"[23] says Bell.

> "I can check these kids up on social media, and I do. And I've not asked for an interview and I've not hired someone because of what I saw on social media."[23]
>
> —Sue Bell, who co-owns Melissa and Sue Camps

## Preparing for a Job Interview

Most employers interview potential employees before offering them a job. The interview can be over the phone or in person. Sometimes, an employer will interview a potential employee right when the person turns in his or her job application. Jodi Sperling is the vice president and director of overnight camps for the JCC (Jewish Community Center) Association. In her role, she hires many teens for jobs with the camps. "The interview is crucial for us," says Sperling. "We're hiring people who are the best role models for our kids, so we want staff who are confident, happy, and warm. If someone can't convey that in an interview, we won't hire them."[24]

Interviewing for a job can be stressful, especially when it is your first time being interviewed. You might feel anxious or nervous. Preparing for the interview in advance can help you feel more confident and surer of yourself.

To prepare for a job interview, you can review typical interview questions and think about how you would answer them. While

## Getting Started as a Social Media Influencer

Social media influencers get paid to share links on their social media accounts. In order to get paid to promote products or services, they must have a large social media following. To get started in this job, you'll need to establish your niche and build your followers on your social media accounts. As an influencer, you will post content in your niche, so make sure to choose something you are interested in and enjoy. You'll need to develop a content strategy—are you only going to post content about your niche interest, or will you mix in content from your personal life or other areas? Once you've decided what type of content you want to post, you'll need to create engaging and interesting content and post it regularly.

As you post content, you should engage with followers as they leave comments. Another way to engage with followers is to ask a question and start a conversation about something of interest. These interactions will help build connections with your followers and solidify your status as an influencer. Once you've built your social media accounts and followers, reach out to brands and let them know you are interested in collaborating. You can add this info to your bio, message and pitch potential brand partners, and visit influencer platforms to find brands in your niche who are open to collaborating. Becoming an influencer takes time and doesn't happen overnight. However, if you keep working at it, you can make money online.

you don't need to memorize your answers, knowing what you want to talk about can help you feel more confident. Conduct a practice interview with a parent or friend playing the role of the potential employer. They can ask you interview questions, and you can practice giving answers, making eye contact, using good body language, and thinking quickly. By role-playing the interview in a safe environment, you'll be a lot more confident when it is time for the real one. Bell says:

I think my advice to a teenager would be to spend some time prior to the interview and just really thinking about themselves and why they are awesome and why they are great. And think of specific reasons, and reasons that set them apart from other people. Not that they're better or worse, just different. Why are you different and why would I want to spend my time with you? Or why would you be a great role model? And with all of those characteristics in your heart and in your head, you're going to walk in confident because you know what makes you awesome. And then you're going to be able to have an interview where you feel confident with what you can bring to this job."[25]

You can also prepare before the interview by gathering the necessary paperwork that you will need to bring, such as a work permit, résumé, and references. Learn everything you can about the business and the position before the interview. Often the job posting will tell you what skills the company wants in an employee and what you should emphasize in an interview. The company's website can provide good information about the business and help you develop some good questions for the interviewer about the job.

The more prepared you are, the better impression you will make on the hiring manager. Maureen Crawford Hentz, who hired teens for specific jobs at the New England Aquarium, often tested teen applicants' interview preparation. "If an applicant came in to interview for an Aquarium Guide position and told me that she thought she would be feeding the animals and 'stuff' I knew that she had not read the job description,"[26] Hentz says.

## Acing the Interview

First impressions count. Make sure you look presentable and clean for your interview. Even if the position is a casual job at an ice-cream shop, dressing up shows a potential employer that you

are serious about work. Unless you are applying for an office job or an internship, you don't need to wear a suit. Business casual outfits such as a clean pair of khaki pants or dress pants and a collared shirt or sweater are good choices. Items you should not wear include low-cut tops, miniskirts, baggy or saggy pants, sneakers, or flip-flops.

Also, on the day of the interview, don't be late. If you can't be on time to an interview, the employer will wonder how reliable you will be as an employee. Instead, try to be about fifteen minutes early. You can use the extra time to review the interview questions and think about your answers.

Once the interview begins, be conscious of your body language. Don't fidget with a pen, jiggle your foot, or play with your hair. Sit still and straight and make eye contact with the interviewer. Bell says:

> Eye contact is our number one. I sometimes just want to look at the person I'm interviewing and say, "You know what, let's take two. Come back and just look at us in the eye. It doesn't even matter what's coming out of your mouth as much as it is that you're just connecting with us." And so when they do walk in with a big smile, shake our hands—which is not often a teenage thing that they do put out their hand right away—shake it, look in the eyes with a big smile, immediately we're relaxed, which makes a great interview.[27]

It's normal to feel nervous during the interview, but you want the interviewer to see you as calm and confident. Julie Lemna, co-owner of Westpark Printing in Boise, Idaho, looks to hire teens who ask questions during an interview. "I look for somebody who has a positive attitude and who verbally communicates,"[28] she says. Sperling recommends that teens put away their cell phone during an interview. "This is a big one. Turn your cellphone off and

"I look for somebody who has a positive attitude and who verbally communicates."[28]

—Julie Lemna, co-owner of Westpark Printing in Boise, Idaho

put it away. Don't leave it out where you might be tempted to look at it during the interview,"[29] she says.

When the interview is over, thank the interviewer for his or her time. Make sure you get the person's business card or other contact information. Within two days, send the interviewer a thank-you note via email. The note should be brief and thank the person for taking the time to interview you, and it should reexpress your interest in the job and in working for the business. Sending a follow-up thank-you can help you stand out from other potential employees and leave the employer with a positive impression of you.

# Chapter Four

# Hired!

The phone rings. You've got the job! Now what? When an employer offers you a job, there are several important pieces of information that you should know. To start, how much will you be paid? Most teen workers are paid an hourly wage for every hour they work. You should compare the job's hourly wage against the minimum wage. In the United States the federal minimum wage is the lowest wage that employers can legally pay their employees. In addition, some states have a minimum wage that is higher than the federal minimum wage. In a few cases, employers are legally allowed to pay an employee less than minimum wage if part of their compensation comes from tips, as long the hourly wage plus the average earned from tips equals the minimum wage. For example, many servers in restaurants earn an hourly wage that is less than minimum wage, but they also earn a portion of their pay from customer tips.

In a few cases, an employer will offer a salary, which is a set amount of earnings per week that does not depend on the number of hours worked. Other times, when a teen is hired to complete a specific project such as building a website or mowing a lawn, he or she may be paid in a fixed, lump sum amount.

Some part-time and summer jobs offer benefits or perks. Retail employees may get discounts at their store, while restaurant staff may get discounts or free meals. Amusement park employees may receive free passes to enjoy the park

## Average Teen Salary Per Hour by State

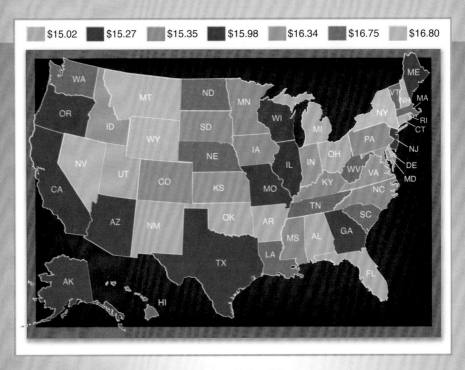

| $15.02 | $15.27 | $15.35 | $15.98 | $16.34 | $16.75 | $16.80 |

Source: ZipRecruiter Inc. 604 Arizona Avenue, Santa Monica, California 90401, USA www.ziprecruiter.com.

on their days off. In some cases, a few employers like Walmart, Starbucks, Chipotle, and UPS offer a full benefits package, including health insurance, to part-time employees. For example, at Chipotle, part-time employees are eligible for tuition reimbursement up to $5,250 per year for college, as well as medical, dental, and vision insurance packages. All of these perks should be included when you are evaluating a job offer and deciding whether it is the right job for you.

## Let's Get Started

Once you've accepted a job offer, there are a few details you'll have to settle. First, you'll discuss your start date and schedule with your supervisor. Many teens have a variety of activities and commitments, from sports to youth groups. It's a good idea to be up front and honest with your supervisor about anything that may conflict with work. Do you have hockey practice every Wednesday afternoon? Tell your manager so that you are not scheduled during those hours. "Scheduling can be tough for an employer and for teenage employees who have multiple priorities like sports and schoolwork," says Lisa Barrow, owner of Kada Recruiting in Summerville, South Carolina. When her own teenage son Tyler got his first part-time job, she advised him to be flexible about work shifts but to be honest with his supervisor about which days or times he could not work. "Before he

## Dealing with Difficult People

Learning how to deal with difficult people is a valuable skill. Whether it is a demanding boss or angry customer, teens will encounter a challenging person at some point at work. If you find yourself face-to-face with a difficult person, try to stay calm. If you need to, take several deep breaths and slowly exhale to calm yourself. No matter how a person is behaving, being rude will not make the situation better. Instead, you should strive to be respectful and polite. Sometimes, listening can make a big difference. Focus on what the other person is saying and try to see his or her point of view. Is there anything you can do to resolve the situation? If you can't take care of the problem yourself, assure the person that you will find a coworker or supervisor nearby who can help.

When dealing with a difficult person who is confronting you, it is natural to want to defend yourself. However, if the other person is emotional, becoming defensive will not help the situation. Try to remember that the person's emotions may be related to something else, so try not to take it personally. In these situations, sometimes just apologizing and promising to do your best to fix the problem can de-escalate a difficult situation. When the situation is resolved and the difficult person has left, talk it over with a coworker or supervisor. Talking about the situation with another person can help reduce any lingering stress you may feel.

was hired, he told his employer that he would have basketball practice, SAT prep and other school obligations. By being clear, the employer knew the time constraints, and Tyler was in control of his own schedule,"[30] Barrow says.

New employees also have to complete certain paperwork, such as a Form W-4 and a Form I-9. A W-4 is a federal tax form completed by an employee that tells an employer his or her tax situation. This information tells the employer how much federal tax to withhold from an employee's paycheck. An I-9 is a US Citizenship and Immigration Services form that verifies a person's identity and legal authorization to work in the United States.

After getting the job, making a schedule is important to keep organized and on time.

## Become a Valued Employee

Once you start working, you can do several things to make yourself become a valued employee to both your employer and coworkers. Start off on the right foot by being early to work. "Just being on time isn't good enough. You need time to come in and get settled. It's amazing what a few extra minutes does to make you stand out and be considered one of the best employees," says Marty Parker, owner of Throw Nation in Dublin, Ohio, a recreation center that employs teens. And if you can't make it to work because you are sick or have a personal emergency, let a manager know. "Do the trifecta—call, email and text about your emergency," Parker says. "Don't assume that just because you email, your boss will get the message. We are very busy and are not on our computers all the time. If you don't do the trifecta, it's essentially like not letting us know."[31]

At work, you represent the business. That's why it is important that you dress appropriately and follow the company dress code if there is one. If you do not have a specific uniform or dress code to follow, casual clothing is appropriate for most teen jobs. Acceptable casual clothing generally includes clean jeans, shorts, and T-shirts. All clothing should be clean, should not be ripped, and should not have symbols, pictures, or wording that may offend others.

> "Just being on time isn't good enough. You need time to come in and get settled. It's amazing what a few extra minutes does to make you stand out and be considered one of the best employees."[31]
>
> —Marty Parker, owner of Throw Nation in Dublin, Ohio

It may sound simple, but make an effort to speak clearly to customers, coworkers, and supervisors. Many teens mumble, speak too softly, or speak too quickly. You might find yourself talking faster when you are uncomfortable or in a new situation. If you are doing this, you might find customers or coworkers

## Stop the Interruption

Few things annoy a supervisor more than being interrupted when talking to a customer or completing an important task. Good employees learn quickly what questions can wait until a later, less busy time. For example, you can hold off asking whether you can leave early or how to fill out a form until your supervisor is not busy assisting customers or gathering financial information for his or her boss. However, good employees recognize when something is urgent, such as an injured team member or customer. In these serious situations, you may need to politely interrupt and pull your supervisor aside to discreetly tell him or her the urgent information. However, in most situations, it is better to be patient and wait until your supervisor has finished his or her conversation.

asking you to repeat yourself. Because good communication skills are important in any job, make an effort to speak slowly and clearly. Practice with family and friends until you feel comfortable. Make eye contact when speaking with others and learn to spot nonverbal cues that signal the other person cannot understand what you are saying.

Another part of good communication is being able to listen well. No matter what job you have, you need excellent listening skills to follow instructions, answer customer questions, and interact with coworkers. Listening also includes paying attention to another person, no matter how the person is conveying information to you. Good employees will make eye contact with people talking to them, instead of staring at the floor or wall. Making eye contact shows others that you are listening and paying attention to them. If you have any questions, wait to ask them until the other person has finished speaking so that you ensure you understand the person's instructions.

Macy Williams, an editorial assistant with the lifestyle website POPSUGAR, advises teen workers to take care with every task on the job, no matter how small. Supervisors will notice and appreciate your effort, she says. Williams explains:

> I was 16 years old when I got my first job as a busser at a locally owned restaurant in my hometown. I was clearing tables, seating guests, making milkshakes, and cleaning up after closing time. It seems like small mindless tasks, but every little thing counts. I learned that you can't get lazy with those little things. It's when you put your all into everything you do that you truly stand out as an employee. The waiters and managers take notice—you will be rewarded for attention to detail. Your superiors really appreciate the simple extra steps you take to make everyone's job easier.[32]

## Master the Soft Skills

No matter what job you have, you can develop essential skills that will make you a valued employee now and in the future. In recent years many employers have complained that entry-level workers in all fields do not have the necessary "soft" skills they need to succeed. Unlike hard skills, which are job-specific knowledge, soft skills are the way a person interacts with others and behaves on the job. Soft skills include motivation, confidence, flexibility, teamwork, negotiation, respect, responsibility, communication, and more.

Anna Roberts, an associate food editor with POPSUGAR, says that her first job as a teenager helped her develop soft skills that she uses in her career today. "I worked at a cafe/bakery as a cashier in high school. From ages 15–18, I worked every day after school and on Sundays. I really learned to

"It's when you put your all into everything you do that you truly stand out as an employee."[32]

—Macy Williams, an editorial assistant with POPSUGAR

break out of my shell and communicate effectively with all sorts of people and work in a fast-paced environment. The skills I learned at that first job have been invaluable. Taking on that much responsibility and developing good work ethic has helped me for every job since,"[33] she says.

According to a Cengage survey released in January 2019, more employers responded that they were looking for employees who possess soft skills (65 percent) as compared to computer skills (47 percent) and other technical skills (50 percent). According to the survey, the top soft skills valued by employers include listening skills, attention to detail, effective communication skills, critical-thinking skills, interpersonal skills, and the ability to learn new skills. "These results show that we must not underestimate the power of the people factor in the workforce. Technology and automation will continue to change and replace jobs, but there are skills that cannot be automated, such as the ability to think critically or problem solve," says Michael Hansen, chief executive officer of Cengage. "There is a need for more soft skills training, both in college and on the job, and today's learners and graduates must continue to hone their skills to stay ahead."[34]

Nariq Richardson from Providence, Rhode Island, spent the summer before his senior year of high school working in an internship for a local construction company. While he learned technical skills specific to his job, Richardson also found he developed valuable soft skills. "That was my first real, paying job. I was really nervous, but I gained a lot of confidence,"[35] he says. Richardson learned that he excelled at multitasking, working with a team, and problem solving. Now he's thinking about pursuing a career in the construction industry, where he could use those skills—maybe as a project manager or architect.

# Chapter Five

# Getting Paid and Paying Taxes

When you have a job, how you get paid depends on whether you are an employee of a business or are self-employed and work for yourself. The distinction between employee versus self-employed also matters when it comes time to pay taxes.

## Getting Paid as an Employee

When you are hired as an employee of a business, you receive a regular paycheck. Some employers pay weekly, while others pay biweekly or monthly. Most employers pay their employees via direct deposit, which allows a business to electronically transfer paycheck money directly into employees' checking or savings accounts. To set up direct deposit of your paycheck, you'll have to fill out paperwork that gives your employer your bank and account information.

Even if your paycheck is automatically deposited into your bank account via direct deposit, you will still receive a pay stub that explains the amount of money you made during the pay period, the amount that was deducted from your pay for taxes and other withholdings, and the net amount of take-home pay deposited into your bank account.

DIRECT DEPOSIT CONFIRMATION

Current
$659.16

Year to Date
$3,954.96

Description
TAXABLE
NET PAYMENT

Payment has been direct deposited to your accour

Direct deposit is easy to set up
with an employer and makes
access to your paycheck faster.

## Gross Pay Versus Net Pay

When you were hired, the manager told you that you would
earn $12 per hour. In the last pay period, you worked 20 hours.
So when you checked your bank account on payday, you
expected to see a direct deposit of $240 ($12x20). Instead,
there's a deposit in your account for only $214. Where did the
money go?

The truth is that what you earn (gross pay) is not the same as
what you actually receive in your bank account (net pay). Your
employer deducts taxes and other items from your paycheck,
leaving you with less money to spend or save.

The total amount you earn during a pay period is your gross
pay. It includes wages, commissions, bonuses, and tips. On your
pay stub, there should be a line for gross pay. You should check
each pay stub to make sure the number of hours included in the
check is correct. You can multiply the number of hours worked by
your hourly rate to calculate gross pay.

Each pay period, your employer will make payroll deductions from your gross pay. A payroll deduction is money that an employer withholds from an employee's payroll check. Payroll deductions include taxes, dues, medical insurance contributions, and retirement plan contributions. The amount deposited in your bank account after all of the deductions is your net pay.

## Before-Tax and After-Tax Deductions

Some payroll deductions are subtracted from gross pay before taxes are calculated and deducted. Before-tax deductions reduce taxable income, which is the amount of income that is taxed. Calculating taxes on a smaller income amount allows you to pay less tax. Examples of before-tax deductions include contributions to retirement savings plans, health and dental insurance premiums, and health savings account contributions. If you do not have any of these benefits at your job, your pay stub will not have any before-tax deductions.

After-tax deductions are subtracted from your paycheck after taxes are calculated and withheld. Examples of after-tax deductions include retirement plan loan repayments, wage garnishments, and contributions to Roth retirement plans.

## Tax Withholdings

Employers are legally responsible for withholding several types of taxes from employee paychecks. These taxes include federal income tax, Social Security tax, Medicare tax, and state and local income tax. Employers withhold these taxes from your paycheck and submit them to the appropriate government agency on your behalf.

Federal income tax withholding is calculated on the basis of several factors. These include your income for the pay period, your year-to-date income, and your Form W-4 withholding allowance. You can find more details about your individual tax rate on the Internal Revenue Service (IRS) website. If you do not meet a minimum threshold for income, you do not have to pay federal income tax. If your employer has withheld federal income tax from your paycheck, you may be eligible for a refund when you file your tax return.

Social Security tax and Medicare tax are also withheld from your paycheck. The amounts you pay for Social Security taxes now will count toward your Social Security earnings record, which will be used to determine your future Social Security benefits. "If you look at your own Social Security statement, it will include wages all the way back to that first job in high school,"[36] says Kelley Long, a member of the National CPA Financial Literacy Commission. Your employer will also withhold state and local income tax from your paycheck. State and local tax withholdings vary depending on where you live.

Understanding the tax withholdings and other deductions from your pay stub is an important way to make sure you are receiving the correct pay from your employer and are paying the correct amount of taxes.

## Getting Paid When You're Self-Employed

Some teens are their own bosses. They might have a dog walking or lawn care business. They might be social media influencer or build websites for clients. In these jobs, you don't get a regular paycheck from an employer. Instead, you get paid when your clients pay you.

Some businesses that hire teens for seasonal work classify them as independent contractors. This creates less paperwork for the business, and it is not required to withhold and remit taxes for you. However, if an employer classifies you as an independent contractor and does not withhold taxes from payments it makes to you, you are responsible for paying your own taxes.

## Working for the Family Business

Some teens get a job working for their mom or dad in a family business. While having your parent as your boss may not be ideal, it can be favorable for taxes on your income. If the parent's business is a sole proprietorship or a partnership, the employer parent does not have to withhold Social Security and Medicare taxes from his or her child's paycheck, as long as the child is less than eighteen years old. However, you will still be responsible for income taxes if you earn enough to meet the minimum income threshold.

It is helpful to think of your client's payment as gross pay. That payment is the total income that you earned. Most of the time, you owe taxes on this income. Because self-employed people do not have an employer withholding and remitting taxes for them, they have to do it themselves. If you are self-employed, you generally will have to pay self-employment tax as well as federal, state, and local income tax. Self-employment tax is the employer and employee share of Social Security and Medicare tax payments. If you earn more than $400 in a self-employed job, you'll need to pay self-employment taxes and file a tax return.

The good news is that if you are self-employed or being paid as an independent contractor, you can deduct job-related expenses from your gross income before calculating your taxes. Judy O'Connor, a certified public accountant (CPA) in Miami Shores, Florida, explains, "If you are a contractor, you receive your contract pay and then can deduct any ordinary and necessary business expenses incurred. You're only taxed on your *net earnings*."[37]

"If you are a contractor, you receive your contract pay and then can deduct any ordinary and necessary business expenses incurred. You're only taxed on your *net earnings*."[37]

—Judy O'Connor, a CPA in Miami Shores, Florida

## Taxes for Social Media Influencers

Social media influencers and bloggers have some special considerations when it comes to taxes. Influencers must report any payments from brand partnerships as income. For example, when a brand pays to sponsor a podcast or for created content, the money received counts as income. Influencers should also report products they receive from brands to review—such as a laptop, clothing, or makeup—as income. You report the fair market value of the item as income. Additionally, any money received from advertising should be reported as income.

Influencers can deduct job-related expenses from income before determining their taxable income. Some examples of common business expenses for influencers and bloggers include phones, laptops, giveaway prizes, website expenses, software and apps, office supplies, trademark and copyright fees, and advertising.

If you are self-employed, you'll need to keep good records of the money you earn and any expenses you have. For example, if you mow lawns, you will have expenses for gas and the maintenance of your lawn mower. If you earn money as an internet influencer, you might have expenses for video or computer equipment, office supplies, and website expenses. Documents such as invoices, copies of checks, deposit records, receipts, and credit card statements will help you confirm your income and expenses when it is time to file your tax return.

## Putting Aside Money for Taxes When You're Self-Employed

Are you a spender or a saver? If you're self-employed, you'll have to file a tax return and pay any required taxes yourself. That means you'll need to make sure that you have the money put aside and saved so that you have it when it is time to pay the taxes.

To help them save money, some teens choose to open two bank accounts, a checking account and a savings account. Each time you get paid by a client, you can deposit the money into your checking account and transfer the tax money to your savings account. That way, you won't spend it, and it will be there when you need to pay it. "I recommend that 50 percent of each paycheck go directly into the teen's savings account, keeping in mind that this may be the only time in their life where it's easy to save money,"[38] says Laura Braziel, a licensed professional counselor who specializes in working with teens and parents.

"I recommend that 50 percent of each paycheck go directly into the teen's savings account, keeping in mind that this may be the only time in their life where it's easy to save money."[38]

—Laura Braziel, a licensed professional counselor who specializes in working with teens and parents

## Savings Goals

Now that you have income, whether as an employee or a self-employed worker, what are your savings goals? Do you have

*Opening a savings account is a great way to save for the future, such as buying a car, college, or getting an apartment.*

something specific that you want to save up to buy? Or are you saving for something bigger in the future, like college or a car? David Young, a CPA in New York, recommends that parents sit down with teens to discuss their savings and spending plans. Young says:

> I would sit down with your teen and say, hey—this is how much is coming in from your paycheck, and how much you're going to set aside. In the case of my son, he's starting college, so how much you're going to need for college. But any teen, he or she is going to have some spending money, some for fun money, gas money getting them back and forth to the job, and this is a great opportunity to show them some basics of budgeting. This is a great opportunity to lay a super foundation for a young person. And this is something that can carry through their whole life, if they understand the idea of budgeting, saving and just how to manage their money well. This is a really good life lesson that can carry through their entire career.[39]

# Chapter Six

# Filing a Tax Return

Your first job can be an exciting experience. You've gained some independence, and your wallet holds a little more money. Now that you have a job and have been earning income, do you need to file a tax return? "I had no idea I had to file my taxes until a friend mentioned it when we got our W-2 forms," says Madison Sero, a fifteen-year-old retail worker. "It's pretty intimidating. I don't know where to start."[40]

Every year, millions of Americans file tax returns with the federal, state, and local governments. Yet not everyone needs to file a tax return. In fact, many teens who work part time do not need to file because their income does not meet the IRS minimum threshold. "Most teenagers working their first summer job won't earn enough money to end up owing any federal income tax at the end of the year,"[41] says Dan Thomas, a CPA and personal financial specialist in Orange County, California. However, you may choose to file a tax return because of other benefits.

> "I had no idea I had to file my taxes until a friend mentioned it when we got our W-2 forms. It's pretty intimidating. I don't know where to start."[40]
>
> —Madison Sero, a fifteen-year-old retail worker

Not every part-time job creates enough income to need to file taxes. Always check with a professional to see whether filing a return is necessary.

## Dependent Status

Whether you need to file a tax return depends on three basic factors: income, filing status, and whether anyone claims you as a dependent. First, are you considered a dependent by the IRS? Most teens who work are dependents, which means that another taxpayer—usually your parents—reports you on their tax returns. When your parents report you as a dependent on their tax return, they can claim certain credits and deductions. "Dependent students may want to have their parents claim them instead of claiming themselves," says Walt Minnick, a financial aid specialist at Orange Coast College. "The tax benefits are usually higher for the parents than for the student, which can better benefit the family as a whole."[42]

To qualify as a dependent, you must either be under age nineteen, a full-time student under age twenty-four, or permanently disabled. You are also a dependent if you live with your parents or caregivers for more than 50 percent of the year and do not provide more than half of your own financial support. If you are considered a dependent for tax purposes, your parents can claim you on their tax returns, and you may not need to file a separate tax return. However, if you earn enough income and do not file a separate tax return, your parents are responsible for the tax you owe.

> "Most teenagers working their first summer job won't earn enough money to end up owing any federal income tax at the end of the year."[41]
>
> —Dan Thomas, a CPA and personal financial specialist in Orange County, California

## How Much Did You Earn?

What type of income and how much did you earn during the year? There are two main types of income: earned and unearned. Earned income is money earned from a job in wages, salary, bonuses, and tips. If you are self-employed or work as an independent contractor, the money you earn is earned income. If you have a business that you actively participate in, the money you earn from it is also considered earned income. Unearned income is income from investments, interest, or dividends.

Here's a quick test to see whether you need to file an income tax return based on your income (based on 2019 minimum income thresholds).

- Do you have unearned income of more than $1,100?
- Do you have earned income greater than $12,200?
- Is your gross income (earned income plus unearned income) greater than the larger of $1,100 or earned income plus $350?
- Do you have self-employment income of more than $400?

If you know that you won't be able to meet the April 15 filing deadline, you can file for an extension. To get an extension, you must file a Form 4868, Application for Automatic Extension of Time to File U.S. Individual Income Tax Return. You must also estimate your tax liability on this form and pay any amount due by the April 15 deadline. If you owe taxes and do not pay them when you file for an extension, you will be charged interest and penalties on the outstanding amount. An extension typically pushes the filing deadline back six months until October 15.

If you answered yes to any of these four questions, you must file a federal income tax return and will probably have to file state and local income tax returns. Even if you do not have to file a federal tax return, you should check the rules of your state and local community to see if you still need to file state and local income tax returns. Also, the minimum income threshold for filing a tax return can change from year to year. You should check the IRS website to see the most up-to-date thresholds for the current year.

Even if you do not meet the income minimum to owe income taxes, you still might need to file a tax return if you are self-employed. If you earned more than $400 of self-employment income, you'll need to pay self-employment tax and file a tax return.

## Other Reasons to File

Even if you are not required to file a tax return, you might want to do it. If your employer withheld federal income tax from your paycheck, you might be eligible for a tax refund. You'll have to file a tax return to get it.

You also might want to file a tax return, even if you didn't have taxes withheld, in order to establish an official income record. In the future, an income record could be useful if you want to use it for anything that requires reporting an income, such as applying for a loan or opening certain retirement savings accounts.

## Tax Anxiety Is Natural

Few people enjoy filling out tax forms. Preparing a tax return for the first time may seem intimidating. Emily, a twenty-seven-year-old freelance graphic designer, admits that she procrastinates filing her taxes because she's nervous about making a mistake and afraid that she will owe money. "This is my first year filing as a freelancer," Emily said in 2018. "I was pretty accustomed to the forms from my old corporate job, but this year's are basically like a foreign language to me. . . . I'll probably end up owing money and I really have no cushion in my bank account. I don't know what I'll do if I owe more than a few hundred dollars."[43]

Kayce Hodos, a licensed professional counselor, explains that filing tax returns can cause anxiety in people because it is natural to be afraid of things one cannot control and does not understand. "For most of us who do not have CPA training and expertise, strange terms like W-2, 1099, 1040, Schedule K and all the others send fear up our spines,"[44] Hodos says.

> "For most of us who do not have CPA training and expertise, strange terms like W-2, 1099, 1040, Schedule K and all the others send fear up our spines."[44]
>
> —Kayce Hodos, a licensed professional counselor

## Gather Your Information

To make filling out your tax return as painless as possible, take a few minutes to gather the forms and documents that you will need before you start. These include personal information such as your Social Security number or tax ID number, birth date, and address.

You'll also need to gather information about your income for the year. In January and February, your employers, banks, and financial institutions will start sending you tax forms that you will need for preparing your tax return. Employers that you worked for during the year will send a Form W-2, Wage and Tax Statement. The W-2 shows how much income you earned in the tax year and how much was withheld for taxes.

If you worked as an independent contractor and earned more than $600, the company will send you a Form 1099-MISC. You might also receive tax forms that show how much interest you've earned on your bank account and tax forms that show the dividends, interest and gains that you've earned on investments. If you have paid tuition, you will receive a Form 1098-T that shows how much you paid, as well as any money you received from grants or scholarships. You should receive all of your tax documents by the end of February.

You'll also need to gather and organize other documents that you will need to fill out your tax return, such as expense or donation receipts or bank account statements. It's a good idea to put all of your documents together in a safe place where you can easily find them when it is time to fill out your return.

If you are self-employed, you'll need to gather your business records. Deposit records show how much income you had. Receipts, credit card statements, and check stubs document your business expenses. If you drive for work, you'll need to have mileage records that show how many miles you drove for the job.

## Filling Out Tax Forms

For most people, federal income tax returns, along with most state and local income tax returns, are due on April 15. If that day is on a weekend or holiday, the tax returns are due on the next business day. However, you should double-check the tax

filing deadlines by checking the IRS website and your state and local community tax authority websites. And the sooner you file your tax return, the sooner you can get your refund, if you are eligible for one. Filing early can also eliminate the stress caused by waiting until the last minute to prepare your tax returns. "One of the biggest issues for first-time tax filers is that they wait until the weekend before they are due,"[45] says Mark Kohler, a CPA.

Once you have all your documents, you're ready to fill out your Form 1040 for your federal income tax return. People with complicated taxes may have to fill out additional tax forms or schedules and attach them to their 1040. Most teens only need to fill out the Form 1040.

For many teens, the easiest way to prepare your tax return is to go online and use the IRS's free tax prep software. The IRS also has electronic versions of its paper forms that will automatically perform tax calculations for you. Alternately, you could use a paid tax preparation software or online tools. These software tools take you step-by-step through filling out your tax return and can help you figure out any deductions or credits that you can take. Some people choose to work one-on-one with a tax professional or a tax service to prepare and file their tax returns. Although you have to pay them, you can see how these professionals prepare your taxes, and then you can prepare them the same way in future years. Alternately, if one of your parents is tax savvy, you might ask them to go through the steps of filling out and filing your tax returns with you.

> "One of the biggest issues for first-time tax filers is that they wait until the weekend before they are due."[45]
>
> —Mark Kohler, a CPA

If you are self-employed, you will need to file some additional schedules with your tax return. On Schedule C, Profit or Loss from Business, you will report all the income and expenses from your business. You'll use this information to calculate net income from your business. If you earned more than $400 in net income, you'll also have to complete a Schedule SE for self-employment tax. You'll file these forms with your 1040. Although it may sound confusing, many tax preparation software programs automatically walk you through the process of filling out the schedules

## Tip Income

Many teens work in part-time or summer jobs as servers, lawn mowers, or in other positions in which they receive tips from customers. For these workers, tips are often a significant part of their total income. Tips can be given as cash, added to a credit card payment, distributed from an employer, and shared among employees. According to tax rules, tip income should be counted as taxable income and is subject to federal, state, and local income tax. If you receive tips in your job, you should keep a daily log to accurately record them, so that you can report tip income when you file your income tax return.

that you will need to file as a self-employed worker, making the process as painless as possible.

In addition to a federal return, you may also need to prepare and file state and local tax returns. Often, these forms use the same information that you already used in your federal return. Once you have completed your tax returns, you can file them as directed, either electronically or by mail. If your tax return calculates that you owe additional taxes, you should pay them as directed when you file your tax return. If you are owed a refund, the fastest way to get it is by direct deposit. However, you can also direct the government to mail you a paper check, if you prefer.

## Keep Organized

While preparing and filing tax returns can be a stressful process, if you are organized and break it down into manageable steps, you can make the process a lot less painful. Learning to keep good records and organize your tax documents can save you a lot of time. When it's time to do your taxes next year, you'll be ready. Teen Madison Sero completed her tax forms on time and got a welcome surprise. She was due to receive more than $200 in tax refunds from her part-time retail job. "It was so much easier than I thought, and I feel like I could do this all on my own next year,"[46] she says.

Many people dread tax time and put off preparing and filing their tax returns until the last minute. However, the more you

Keeping all of your financial paperwork organized can help make the tax process easier.

know about your income, taxes, and preparing your returns, the less intimidating the process will be. With a little bit of preparation and organization, you'll realize that taxes are not as scary as you thought. You'll be ready to file at tax time.

You may also want to use a tax service if you are self-employed, like H&R Block. Although you have to pay them, you can copy what they have done for you every year, and you can deduct what you pay them as an expense next year. Or, if you have a parent willing to go through the steps with you, that works too.

# Source Notes

## Introduction: Valuable Experience

1. Quoted in Linda Jacobson, "Students Gain Workforce Skills Through Part-Time Jobs," Education Dive, March 1, 2018. www.educationdive.com.
2. Quoted in Jacobson, "Students Gain Workforce Skills Through Part-Time Jobs."
3. Quoted in Jacobson, "Students Gain Workforce Skills Through Part-Time Jobs."

## Chapter One: Types of Jobs: Where to Start

4. Quoted in Ana Homayoun, "Advice for Teenagers Looking for Summer Jobs," *New York Times*, June 12, 2019. www.nytimes.com.
5. Quoted in Karen Finucan Clarkson, "Help Your Teen Find a Summer Job," *Washington Parent*, January 2018. www.washingtonparent.com.
6. Quoted in Rachel Dotson, "Job Search & Career Advancement: The One Thing You're Probably Missing," ZipRecruiter. www.ziprecruiter.com.
7. Quoted in Lisa Dayley Smith, "East Idaho Teen Starts Lawn Care Business," *Idaho State Business Journal* (Pocatello, ID), April 30, 2019. www.idahostatejournal.com.
8. Quoted in Alison Novak, "Why Did You Choose to Work at a Camp?," Kids VT, April 4, 2017. www.kidsvt.com.
9. Quoted in Ellen Pong, "They Work Hard for the Money," Topic, July 2019. www.topic.com.
10. Quoted in Elinor Florence, "Help Your Teen Get a Summer Job," *Reader's Digest Canada*, 2020. www.readersdigest.ca.

11. Quoted in Alyse Kalish, "5 Skills You Can Use to Transfer into a Sales Career (That You Probably Already Have)," The Muse, 2020. www.themuse.com.

12. Quoted in Elora Tocci, "Advice for Teens Looking to Land a Summer Job," *Hudson Valley Parent*. https://hvparent.com.

13. Quoted in Taylor Lorenz, "Posting Instagram Sponsored Content Is the New Summer Job," *The Atlantic*, August 22, 2018. www.theatlantic.com.

14. Quoted in Lorenz, "Posting Instagram Sponsored Content Is the New Summer Job."

## Chapter Two: The Job Hunt

15. Quoted in OKCollegeStart, "Identifying and Working Your Network." www.okcollegestart.org.

16. Quoted in OKCollegeStart, "Identifying and Working Your Network."

17. Quoted in Risa C. Doherty, "Mistakes Teens Make When Looking for Jobs," *Bay Area Parent*, 2020. www.bayareaparent.com.

18. Quoted in OKCollegeStart, "Identifying and Working Your Network."

19. Quoted in Homayoun, "Advice for Teenagers Looking for Summer Jobs."

20. Quoted in Dennis Darrow, "Pueblo Workforce Center Go-To Place for Summer Jobs Starting with Next Week's Expo," *Pueblo (CO) Chieftain*, April 2, 2019. www.chieftain.com.

21. Quoted in Clarkson, "Help Your Teen Find a Summer Job."

## Chapter Three: Job Application and Interview

22. Quoted in Pamela Kleibrink Thompson, "10 Tips to Manage and Coach Teenage Employees," *Training*, July 19, 2017. https://trainingmag.com.

23. Quoted in Alison Green, "Transcript of 'The Weird World of Interviewing Teenagers,'" Ask a Manager, December 5, 2018. www.askamanager.org.

24. Jodi Sperling, "14 Helpful First Job Interview Tips for Your Teenager," *Your Teen Magazine*, 2019. https://yourteenmag.com.

25. Quoted in Green, "Transcript of "The Weird World of Interviewing Teenagers.'"

26. Quoted in Jacob Share, "Interview Preparation for Teens: 11 Tips for Getting the Job," LiveCareer, 2020. www.livecareer.com.

27. Quoted in Green, "Transcript of "The Weird World of Interviewing Teenagers.'"

28. Quoted in Thompson, "10 Tips to Manage and Coach Teenage Employees."

29. Sperling, "14 Helpful First Job Interview Tips for Your Teenager."

## Chapter Four: Hired!

30. Quoted in Geoff Williams, "What Teens Must Know Before Starting a First Job," *U.S. News & World Report*, May 31, 2019. https://money.usnews.com.

31. Quoted in Williams, "What Teens Must Know Before Starting a First Job."

32. Quoted in Ashley Paige, "13 of the Greatest Lessons We Learned at Our First Jobs," POPSUGAR, September 28, 2017. www.popsugar.com.

33. Quoted in Paige, "13 of the Greatest Lessons We Learned at Our First Jobs."

34. Quoted in Cengage, "New Survey: Demand for 'Uniquely Human Skills' Increases Even as Technology and Automation Replace Some Jobs," January 16, 2019. https://news.cengage.com.

35. Quoted in Sarah Gonser, "How Teens Are Learning Crucial 'Soft Skills' Before Their Internships Start," KQED, November 30, 2018. www.kqed.org.

## Chapter Five: Getting Paid and Paying Taxes

36. Quoted in Kimberly Lankford, "What Kids with Summer Jobs Need to Know About Taxes," *Kiplinger*, May 15, 2015. www.kiplinger.com.

37. Quoted in Kay Bell, "Tax Issues That Impact Working Teens and Their Parents," Bankrate, December 5, 2018. www.bankrate.com.
38. Quoted in Huff Post, "Your Kid Just Got Their First Job. Here's How to Set Them Up Managing Money," February 25, 2019. www.huffpost.com.
39. Quoted in WROC, "Summer Jobs Are More than Just a Paycheck for Teens, CPA Says," WIVB.com, June 11, 2018. www.wivb.com.

## Chapter Six: Filing a Tax Return

40. Quoted in Michelle Argento, "Let's Get Legit About Teens and Taxes," Financial Avenue, March 2, 2017. https://fa.financialavenue.org.
41. Quoted in Lankford, "What Kids with Summer Jobs Need to Know About Taxes."
42. Quoted in Michael Rand, "Tax Guide for College Students," Simple Dollar, March 4, 2020. www.thesimpledollar.com.
43. Quoted in Caitlin Flynn, "Yes, Tax Anxiety Is Real—Here's How to Deal with It," SheKnows, April 8, 2018. www.sheknows.com.
44. Quoted in Flynn, "Yes, Tax Anxiety Is Real—Here's How to Deal with It."
45. Quoted in Anna Bahney, "How to File Your Taxes for the First Time," CNN Money, March 30, 2018. https://money.cnn.com.
46. Quoted in Argento, "Let's Get Legit About Teens and Taxes."

# Glossary

**application:** A paper or online form filled out by job seekers to apply for an open position.

**deductions:** Items subtracted from a paycheck, such as health insurance premiums, or subtracted from taxable income when calculating tax due.

**dependent:** A person (often a child) claimed by another (often a parent) on the other's tax return.

**gross pay:** The total amount of income earned before deductions.

**informational interview:** An interview with a person with the goal of learning more about a particular job or company.

**interpersonal skills:** The behaviors and tactics a person uses to interact with others effectively.

**interview:** An in-person, phone, or online meeting with a potential employer.

**net pay:** The amount of income a worker receives after taxes and other deductions are subtracted.

**networking:** Developing professional relationships with people that may be useful in the future for finding a job.

**reference:** A person who will verify that a job applicant is a responsible person and good worker.

**résumé:** A document that highlights a person's work history, educational experiences, achievements, and skills.

**salary:** Total annual earnings paid to an employee.

**soft skills:** Personal characteristics that help a person function well at work or in a group setting, such as punctuality, attentional to detail, and communication skills.

**wages:** Money paid to workers by the hour.

**withholding:** Taxes taken out of a paycheck.

# For Further Research

## Books

Leanne Currie-McGhee, *Getting a Job*. San Diego: ReferencePoint, 2019.

DK, *The Careers Handbook: The Ultimate Guide to Planning Your Future*. London: DK, 2019.

Robin Ryan, *60 Seconds and You're Hired!* New York: Penguin, 2016.

Beverly Slomka, *Teens and the Job Game: Prepare Today—Win It Tomorrow*. Herndon, VA: Mascot, 2018.

Elissa Thompson and Ann Byers, *Ace Your Résumé, Application, and Interview Skills*. New York: Rosen Central, 2019.

Kathryn Troutman, *Creating Your First Résumé: A Step-by-Step Guide to Write Your First Competitive Résumé*. Catonsville, MD: Federal Career Training Institute, 2016.

Karen Wickre, *Taking the Work Out of Networking: Your Guide to Making and Keeping Great Connections*. New York: Gallery, 2019.

## Internet Sources

Kay Bell, "Tax Issues That Impact Working Teens and Their Parents," Bankrate, December 5, 2018. www.bankrate.com.

Alison Doyle, "Teen Job Interview Questions, Answers, and Tips," Balance Careers, May 26, 2019. www.thebalancecareers.com.

Indeed, "8 Interview Questions for Teens with Examples and Tips," February 25, 2020. www.indeed.com.

Rebecca Lake, "Teens and Taxes: What Parents Need to Know About Summer Jobs," SmartAsset, December 10, 2019. https://smartasset.com.

TaxSlayer, "Taxes for Teens—a Beginner's Guide," February 3, 2020. www.taxslayer.com.

Denise Witmer, "Teens and Income Taxes," The Balance, October 29, 2019. www.thebalance.com.

## Websites

**Resources for Young Workers, US Department of Labor** (www.dol.gov/general/topic/youthlabor/studentworkers). This website has information about age requirements, working in a family business, and other information for workers under age eighteen.

**Tax Information for Individuals, Internal Revenue Service** (www.irs.gov/individuals). The IRS website provides information for individual tax filers on when and how to file taxes and includes a section specifically geared toward students.

***Teens Got Cents*** (www.teensgotcents.com). This blog created by a teen for teens features a variety of financial information geared toward youth, including several articles and features about jobs.

# Index

# Picture Credits

# About the Author

Carla Mooney is the author of many books for young adults and children. She lives in Pittsburgh, Pennsylvania, with her husband and three children. Before becoming an author, Carla applied for and worked in a variety of jobs including babysitter, amusement park worker, catering event server, small business bookkeeper, and financial accountant.